Minimalist:

Your 30 day mental rework guide to a minimalist life, to declutter your home, mind and emotions

By

Beatrice Anahata

The information provided herein is stated to be truthful and consistent, in that any liability, in terms of inattention or otherwise, by any usage or abuse of any policies, processes, or directions contained within is the solitary and utter responsibility of the recipient reader. Under no circumstances will any legal responsibility or blame be held against the publisher for any reparation, damages, or monetary loss due to the information herein, either directly or indirectly.

Respective authors own all copyrights not held by the publisher.

The information herein is offered for informational purposes solely, and is universal as so. The presentation of the information is without contract or any type of guarantee assurance.

The trademarks that are used are without any consent, and the publication of the trademark is without permission or backing by the trademark owner. All trademarks and brands within this book are for clarifying purposes only and are the owned by the owners themselves, not affiliated with this document.

Table of Contents

Chapter 1: Minimalism

True minimalism is quite different from what you see in mainstream media. Many people are leading "minimalist" lifestyles to the extreme, eliminating everything they have from the picture and living with next to nothing. In reality, this is often a delusional depiction of what minimalism truly is. These scenarios are often attention-grabbing for their shock value, and lead people to believe that a minimalist lifestyle means that you live a life of lack and struggle. After all, how joyful can you be when you have nothing to fulfill your day-to-day needs?

If you want to be a true minimalist, you must first understand exactly what minimalism is, and what it isn't. To make it very simple: minimalism means to lead a life whereby you only use what you need for regular basis. Anything and everything else that no longer serves you or brings you joy is either thrown away or given away, thus freeing up space in your physical environment, as well as in your psychological one. To understand this description on a deeper level, we will further explore the concept of minimalism.

What Is True Minimalism?

Being a true minimalist means that you lead a life where you no longer hold on to things that no longer serve you. When you look around your home, you no longer see clutter because everything has a purpose and is used on a regular basis. Anything that no longer has a purpose is eliminated from your life, either by way of trash, donation, or sales. You no longer spend your life collecting and hoarding "treasures" in your home. Instead you live free from the consumerism lifestyle. Your life isn't spent acquiring more stuff; it is spent enjoying life and doing what you want when you want, free of any physical burdens. You release emotional attachments to objects, and you find peace in life itself, instead of in objects that prove to be obsolete over time.

How Do You Benefit?

There are many major benefits that arise from living life as a minimalist. First off, when you eliminate unnecessary clutter from your home, it has a highly therapeutic action on your mind. Right now, look around the room and notice five different items that you would consider to be clutter. Take a moment and truly think about what these objects mean to you. Do they bring you joy or happiness anymore? Or do you hold onto them for some tie to the past that they resemble for you? Or, do you simply hold onto them because you are too proud or too lazy to let them go, so you just do nothing instead? The clutter we store in our houses never comes without consequence. We often feel guilty about these items. We may have buyer's remorse or guilt that we no longer live under the circumstances that we once did when the item came into our home. We may have resentment towards the item for always becoming a source of clutter and stress, instead of simply disappearing and no longer being present to cause this stress. We wish that the item would disappear because the burden of actually having to get rid of it means that we would have to face emotions we don't want to face: guilt, despair, and other difficult emotions. When we get rid of these items, though, we eliminate these emotions altogether.

Aside from the emotional and psychological benefits of removing clutter from our lives, there are other benefits as well. For example, when you have fewer belongings, it becomes easier to maintain them. You no longer spend your entire life cleaning up clutter, because clutter ceases to exist in your life. Everything you own has a purpose, and it has its spot to be stored so that it never gets in the way. It makes life significantly easier. As well, you no longer have to spend your entire life working tirelessly to purchase new stuff and maintain existing stuff. You don't have expenses related to fixing broken objects or acquiring new ones, so you simply have to make enough to afford to live your day-to-day life. You are free to do whatever you want with your spare time, without fear of leaving behind a house full of objects that serve no purpose other than to tie you down and fill your life with stress and misery. You can travel, move, and do virtually anything you desire to do without any attachments to the belongings you own. Case, the thirty-day journey toward adopting a clutter-free minimalist lifestyle starts with the single most crucial step of deciding to carry out the most definitive lifestyle makeover ever.

To many, a minimalist lifestyle denotes a harking back to the times of our cavemen ancestors with little or no access to all the modern amenities that make life worth living. However, the ones who understand the real implications of a minimalist lifestyle realize that its basic premise is that you have a surfeit of what you need to lead a happy and fulfilling life and by thoughtlessly hankering after what you don't have and don't need, you invite needless anxiety and unhappiness.

Before you even begin to take any concrete steps toward adopting a minimalist lifestyle you should hold a clear understanding of what it is not. It does not necessarily mean turning your back on every semblance of the modern way of life. You can lead a clutter-free life without having to make any seemingly appalling sacrifices.

However, you do need to radically change your mindset to the extent that you start valuing yourself above the material things, the acquiring of which you had hitherto made the raison d'etre of your existence. You can do that by dwelling on the benefits of leading a clutter-free minimalist life-

1.   Decluttering sets you free

Once you start getting rid of the substantial number of material possessions that you have been cramming into various parts of your home, you will feel a lot lighter and freer. For one there will be more space in your home, allowing you greater freedom, both in terms of being able to move around more easily and no longer having to take care of so much stuff.

The sense of liberty will not just be a physical one, but also a mental one, in that you will be free of the baggage of the past, enabling you to focus on what matters to you now. To take an extreme example, if you still hoard the toys you played with as a child, wouldn't you feel a lot better, if you gave those away to someone's children who might need them? You are hardly likely to be using those toys again!

2.   Helps you find focus

Having too many possessions dulls your focus. For one, all the property needs to be taken care of, and in many cases where you have bought stuff on credit, there is the added stress of having to pay for it. Isn't it far better to get rid of the bills in one fell swoop and instead focus on the more important things in life like building relationships? Rather than pay the monthly installment toward the fancy sports car, you could perhaps use the money for your children's education.

3. Save money for the important things of life

Rather than splurging on a possession that adds no real value to your life, living a life with less expenditure you could do two things at the same time. One reduces your dependence upon money, and two, get rid of debt the bane of American society.

Imagine a life where you spend as much as it takes to get by and not spend most of your living hours trying to make enough to finance your profligate lifestyle. What is the point of that?

4. You live better

A minimalist lifestyle makes very little demands on your time, and the sense of freedom and lightness that it provides you makes you healthier. Consequently, you get to live a contented life, precisely the way you want to be.

For instance, you may be living a minimalist life with the minimum of possessions, a relatively small workload and plenty of time to spend with your family. The thing about this lifestyle is that it is a choice based one. You can make your life as minimalist as you like. There is no duress involved.

The important thing is that with all the physical and mental clutter gone from your life, you will enjoy better health and have more energy to live your life to the fullest. It is precisely for this reason that minimalism is growing in popularity by the day. More and more people realize that this way of living is the best. It lets you live life the way that it is meant to be in the most simple yet amazingly effective way. It shows you a whole new paradigm of going about your daily existence-the right one.

Get Down to Business

Adopting a minimalist lifestyle is definitely a leap of faith, but if you have decided that it makes sense for you to have one, nothing is to be gained by dilly-dallying or postponing the inevitable. However, you can do this is a manner that makes you feel comfortable, as the whole idea behind leading a minimalist life is to eliminate stress and not create it.

What you can do to feel better about the entire process is to do it in tandem with others who are inclined to adopt the minimalist and clutter-free way of life. It could be close or even distant members of your family, friends, and colleagues. You could get together and start a thirty-day contest about who gets rid of most clutter on a day to day basis for a period of thirty days, at the end of which you can decide a winner on the basis of who is most successful in getting rid of most stuff.

The game could easily be made more interesting by making the rate of getting rid of unwanted possessions a progressive one. For instance, the first day you could start with one item, the second day with two things, the third day with three items and so on till the thirtieth day when each one of you will have to get rid of a whopping thirty items!

As you can imagine the game might be quite easy initially, but will soon become increasingly difficult to play. Think of what all you can get rid of, clothes, furniture, decoration pieces, electronic equipment, kitchenware, old books, footwear, bottles, cans and so much more. You could donate, sell or throw away the extra stuff lying at home, but the idea is to keep to the schedule.

As you progress through the days, you will realize how much unnecessary stuff you had been holding on and how with each disposal you somehow feel a little lighter and freer. There will be those among you who will be very loath to let go of some of the stuff but will eventually see the wisdom in removing past deadwood. Some of you will not be able to bear the sense of loss or separation and may drop out of the contest, way before it reaches a conclusion.

By the time you reach the end of thirty days, you will likely have not only got used to living with far less possessions than before, but actually seen that it wasn't as difficult as you had imagined that it would be. Not only that you would have begun to experience the benefits of leading a minimalist life. If any of your fellow contestants too make it, you will feel elated in their company and if they haven't, you can thank them for giving it their best shot and helping you in your journey toward a new more fulfilling lifestyle. For all you know they might reconsider their decision to leave the field and return to the fold someday.

Decluttering of your life, of course, comprises of much more than getting rid of some odd possessions. It has much more to get rid of the whole paradigm of the avaricious-materialistic-perennial-growth driven approach to life. An approach that would have you forever chase the chimera of worldly success without allowing you to pause to reflect upon what you actually want from life.

Thirty Days to Prepare

A minimalist lifestyle is not only about getting rid of material possessions. It has to do far more with mentally letting go of your attachment to a thoroughly materialistic lifestyle. You will most likely find it harder to manage the latter rather than the former, especially in the first thirty days of your attempted makeover. That is why you will have to undergo this process a day at a time. Given below is a thirty-day plan of action that lets you both test the waters and ease into a clutter-free minimalist lifestyle

1. *Don't Go Online*- We have started living our lives more in the virtual world than the real world thanks to the technology revolution. If possible, this has made our lives even more disconnected with what is truly important for us. The very term virtual reality is a giveaway in that it is not real. How can anything that is not real, provide us with lasting happiness?

Try going completely offline for a day and get a sense of a different kind of freedom, where you are not bombarded with information about the goings on in the far corners of the materialistic world. Neither do you feel the pressure to keep up with your hundreds possibly thousands of Facebook friends who should not really mean a thing to you?

Instead, you could try meeting up with your real friends who you know would always stand by you. Focus on enjoying the meal that you are eating, rather than snapping it with your smartphone and posting a picture to be liked on social media!

2. Reduce your digital dependence- Now that you have a fair idea about the advantages of spending more of your time in the real world than in the digital one go ahead and reduce your dependence upon the latter. One realizes that you may not be immediately able to get off the grid, but you can sure restrict your access to it.

You can do this by checking your emails, texts, and social media messages just once in a day. Simultaneously stop posting on social media, if not deactivate the accounts. Don't keep multiple devices that keep you hooked to the Internet. Instead of making most of your purchases online, start visiting stores. This will not only let you see and feel, what you are buying, but also interact and connect with the sales people. Getting out of the pernicious digital ivory tower will do your body and soul a world of good.

3. Take up meditation- For you to get away from the attractions of a consumerist and materialistic world, you need to be able to connect with your own innermost thoughts and feelings and find out what it is that you actually want. A profound way of doing that is by taking up meditation.

It has repeatedly been stated, and scientifically proven that meditation has immense physical and mental health benefits. By calming you down, it stops the flow of a whole lot of extraneous and adverse thoughts passing through your mind and lets you have a rare clarity about what really matters to you. This will help you understand how a minimalist lifestyle firmly puts you on the permanent path to peace, tranquility and real progress.

4. Give up cribbing- We have all been fed on a constant diet for striving for more than we have and indeed need. What this does is programs us to crib and be dissatisfied with what we have. How sick is that?

We have to stop cribbing ceaselessly and be grateful for the great gift of life and cherish every moment of it. Ending the need to crib is not always as easy as it might appear, as we are so used to demanding more and more and more. Once you snap out of this habit, you will begin to realize, how truly blessed you are already and instead of cribbing you will learn to savor what you have.

5. Take to reading- Reading has taken a backseat in today's times what with myriad entertainment options available online. Nothing exemplifies a minimalist lifestyle better than reading. There is nothing ostentatious about reading, yet there is a wealth of knowledge to be acquired here.

Spend time learning the wisdom of the world by reading instead of splurging your wealth on gadgets and gizmos which you will probably not use half the time. Reading, on the other hand, is inexpensive but can keep you absorbed for hours.Though it's possible that you might not be able to keep up with the Joneses by indulging in this activity, but then you will need to for you would have found yourself.

6. *Prioritize-* Take an entire day to figure out what you want to truly achieve in life. Is it the unmindful pursuit of one material goal after the other or is it doing the best for your family by providing ensuring that they lead a happy, content and healthy life?

You have got to choose between ceaseless hankering after materialistic goals which add no value to your life or choose a lifestyle that enables you to live your life at a deeper level.

Do you want to be beset with lifestyle diseases or would you rather live a simple and robust life?

7. Make the right commitments- The commitments you make in life determine how much you are in tune with a minimalist lifestyle. If you are committed to attending a party every weekend, you can forget about adopting it. On the other hand, if reducing the carbon footprint weighs upon your mind, you are on the right track, in so far as adopting a minimalist lifestyle is concerned.

8. Make a fresh start in the mornings- Even though a minimalist lifestyle is all about uncomplicating your life, it does require for you to introduce a modicum of discipline to your life. Starting your mornings with an invigorating ritual like a brisk walk, yoga or going for a run would help you focus your thoughts and channelize your energy in a positive and fruitful direction.

9. Eating Sensibly- Somebody has rightly said that we are what we eat and a minimalist lifestyle would have you eat simple and sensible meals. You wouldn't be expected to gorge on lifestyle disease inducing processed food, high in sugar and fat content.

Simple, nutritious food like whole grains, fresh fruits and vegetables and fish will keep you both healthy and fit. Besides, you will not end up spending a fortune on them

10. *Learn to enjoy solitude*- Nobody knows you better than you yourself. Spend time with yourself in solitude, and you will discover that it takes very little for you to be happy.

11. *Stop Wasting*- Our modern consumerist lifestyle generates an appalling amount of waste- discarded food, empty bottles, clothes that we buy and never wear, electronic junk and so on and so forth. You have to begin opting out and the time is now.

12. *Use public transport*- That fact that most of us go about in our personal vehicles might be very convenient for us but puts inordinate strain on the planet's scarce natural resources. Besides, it makes us lazy and fat.

Start using public transport instead. It will both reduce your carbon footprint and make you fitter in that you will have to walk to the bus or subway station.

13. *Shop sensibly*- There are so many enticing clothes, jewelry, accessories, cosmetics,

electronic gadgets and a wealth of other objects of desire that tie us to a world of excess. Break free by shopping sensibly only for what you really need.

14. Plan ahead- Living a minimalist life is something that you have to commit to long term. You need to plan ahead for the entire year so that you know what exactly you are getting into and what it is that you are required to give up. Besides, you will have to learn to live your life in ways that are very different from before.

15. Learn to not buy- Minimalist living is all about your having to buy as little as possible. Most of our needs are easily met, and we have to get out of the habit of buying something or the other every day. Stop yourself from buying anything in the next twenty-four hours to prepare yourself for a whole new way of living.

16. Don't multitask- Get out of the bad habit of multitasking. Far from achieving more, you end up losing focus on everything you take up simultaneously. Instead, learn to be absorbed with one task at a time and do it with all sincerity.

17. Start keeping a gratitude journal- There is so much to be thankful for in life, and one best practice to accomplish that is to start keeping a gratitude journal. Start noting down instances for which you should express gratitude, and you will realize how happy you are.

18. Stop indulging in one-man-up ship- Life is not about showing others that you are the boss. This may get you temporary gains in the corporate world, but make you deeply unhappy inside. Give up this bad habit and be good to others, so that they are good to you.

19. Work on identifying and removing stress triggers- All of us have stress triggers which keep us from being happy all the time. The minimalist lifestyle encourages you to understand your stress triggers and work toward eliminating them.

20. Spend a day that is entirely unplanned- While discipline and following a set daily schedule makes sense, there can be a day set aside that is completely unplanned. This is in acknowledgment of the fact that we are not machines or robots, but human beings with free will. See how the day unfolds in the most unexpectedly interesting ways.

21. Give up a goal - We have made our lives so miserable in pursuit of so many goals. Try giving up a goal and see how liberating that can be. If you can't into a dress size that you easily did twenty years ago, accept that fact and put on something that suits you instead.

22. Analyze your last five purchases - We are so used to cluttering our lives with useless stuff that we pick up almost on a daily basis that we do not even realize, how this phenomenon has trapped us in this never-ending phenomenon of buying for the sake of buying. Analyze your purchases of the last five days, and you will be astounded at how much of it was unnecessary.

23. Reclaim your sleep - In our quest for success we are willing to sacrifice so much, even a good night's sleep. Once we realize that the journey we were following was an unwise one, we can focus on better ones. Like following a daily routine that exercises our body and relaxes our mind enough to make us fall asleep without much trouble.

24. Lend a helping hand to someone - We need to take a break from the cut-throat world of our workplace where self-interest dominated everything else. Medical science tells us, this is bad for our health. Try to help someone every day. It will bringer and stronger and brighter feeling as you go along.

25. *Reconnect with nature-* We are the children of nature and get rejuvenated in its bosom. Get out of your artificial cocooned existence more often. Start with a day-long trip to a lakeside or a riverfront. Recharge your batteries by becoming a part of nature once again and not its adversary.

26. *Learn to share-* Our natural resources are scarce. Learn to share them. Become part of a carpool and share your daily ride to office and back with someone.

27. *Become more social-* Keep your smartphone at home and try engaging people in conversations at public places-at the shopping mall, airport, and restaurant. Reconnect with real people.

28. *Stop using disposable products-* Stop your dependence upon disposable things. Water bottles, food packaging, plastic cups, disposable tissue and so much more which is rendering our planet toxic.

29. *Reuse and reuse*- Instead of using and throwing things, start using and reusing them. Don't drink water from a paper cup, use a proper glass instead. Buyer fewer clothes and wash them more often. You can start making these changes to your lifestyle so as to be able to seamlessly adopt a minimalist way of life.

30. *Give up automation*- Most of the gadgets that we use at home are actually adding nothing to our lives and only making us lazy, fat and unwell. Try to stop using your washing machine, microwave oven, dishwasher and vacuum cleaner and do the cleaning and washing manually. It might be challenging work, but you will be fitter and healthier for it.

Do You Have to Get Rid of Everything?

Being a minimalist doesn't mean you are getting rid of everything you have. Instead, it means that you are getting rid of everything that no longer serves you. If you love painting, for example, by all means, keep your painting supplies. But if you don't love painting and you simply keep the supplies around "just in case you'll use them one day," then it is time to get rid of them. If you were going to use them, you would have by now. And, if you decide to pick up a paint brush in the future, you can simply purchase new supplies or even attend a painting class instead of acquiring all of the supplies and soon just have them stored.

Anything that actively serves a purpose in your life can and should be kept. However, anything that is only kept out of obligation or fear of not having it when you need it should be eliminated. The truth is, we can easily acquire new things when we find we need them in our lives. There is no sense carrying around a large selection of items that we no longer need, especially when we are not using them. That is when your belongings become clutter, and your clutter becomes stressful, and your life becomes miserable. If you want to make a change, you have to learn to eliminate what no longer serves you and keep what does.

Can You Ever Shop Again?

Of course, you can! Minimalism doesn't mean that you will never shop or make purchases again. It simply means that you must learn to be more mindful about what you are bringing into your house. If you are purchasing objects that you know you will not use for longer than a few days or weeks, then it is likely a better idea to overlook that object completely. Worst case scenario, see if you can rent one or borrow to a friend to see if you actually like the object. If not, then simply don't invest your money, time or space into acquiring the object. Instead, move on!

Where Is the Joy in All of This?

The greatest sense of joy that you will acquire from the minimalist lifestyle is the freedom. You no longer have to work twice as hard to acquire things and maintain them. Instead, you can reduce the amount of effort you put into things by purchasing less clutter and storing less clutter. You save a large amount of time this way, and you provide yourself with the opportunity to do virtually anything you desire. Instead of being stuck in the consumerism cycle, you can begin to enjoy life itself genuinely. You can start experiencing life as it is, free of any physical thing that holds you down. You will no longer feel obligated to invest so much time in maintaining and protecting your belongings, and it will be easier for you to pack things up and move along. You can move, travel, and do virtually anything you want without fear of being held back by your physical items. As well, you will have more free time due to not having to work as hard to have what you have.

Minimalism is not quite like what they tell you it is in mainstream media. It isn't about living in an extreme state of lack, where you have virtually nothing in your life. There is no rule that says you can only own a set number of items or only certain things can be kept if you are going to be a true minimalist. You can own any number of things and be a true minimalist. The key is making sure that all of those items are valuable, and that you will use them for an ongoing period. As long as the intention behind your belongings is proper, then you can consider yourself a true minimalist.

Remember, the journey is about bringing joy and freedom. The process of eliminating your belongings and freeing up your physical space and your psychological and emotional space is not about creating a new and different situation that brings stress and discomfort. It is about relieving stress and discomfort altogether and learning to live life in a way that is more fulfilling and satisfying to you. It is about bringing freedom, happiness, and joy together in your life by no longer being trapped in the consumerism cycle, and learning to live a life that is no longer bound by physical belongings that don't even serve you. When you learn to live life like a true minimalist, then you will be able to enjoy all of the many values that life has to offer, the true minimalist way. If you are ready to start living life like this, then you are ready to commence day one of your 30-day minimalist challenge.

Chapter 2: Days 1 to 10

The first ten days of minimalism are going to be some of the hardest. In this time, you are going to start eliminating things from your life and learning to live in a whole new way. You may feel a variety of emotions at this time; the experience will be unique to you. If you must, take your time and do it slowly. The purpose of this challenge is to successfully teach you to practice minimalism with a comfortable transformation, not to shock you into a new lifestyle that will leave you with regret and misery over the choices you have made. Practice each day as it is provided and you will realize how simple the transition can be and how rewarding liberation from a physical tie can be, as well.

Day 1

The very first day of your challenge is going to start out simple. You want to collect a box which you will keep in a central location in your house. Then, you will place one item in there that you wish to donate. For the next thirty days, you will continue to place one single item into this box. This is an easy task that will allow you to eliminate thirty items from your home that you no longer need.

By doing it just one at a time, you make it extremely simple for you to let go of these items, as you have a full 24 hours to process the idea that these items will be gone for good. There are two challenges in this act: first, you are not to remove anything from the donation bin. Once it's in there, it must stay there. Second, you must only work one at a time. The idea is not to get overwhelmed or shocked by jumping into a new lifestyle. It can be hard to see your entire home change rapidly, even if you have wished for it to happen for a long time. If you move too quickly, you may regret your actions and end up purchasing several items to replace what you no longer have within' your home. The goal is to learn how to live without these items, one at a time.

As a bonus task for day one, you might want to take a journal you already have lying around your home, or take to the notepad on your computer and start writing d your experience as you work through this process. Writing out how you are feeling each day will help you process the changes you are making. Then, when you potentially reach a point of struggle, you can return to your writing and read why you made the changes you did. Be sure to share how you felt before you started the challenge and the intimate reasons as to why you started the challenge in the first place. This will help set you up for success if you ever find you reach a point where it is becoming difficult for you. Once you have done this, you have completed your day 1 activities for the 30-day challenge.

Day 2

"Out of sight, out of mind" is a phrase we know all too well in life. When we collect clutter, we often shove it aside into places where we can no longer see it so that we don't have to regularly revisit the guilt and regret we feel around investing our time and money into these items. When we do this, however, we do not face the problem head on. Instead, we sweep it under the rug and pretend there is no problem, to begin with.

For day two, you are going to sort through your junk drawer, or junk drawers if you have many. You are going to get rid of everything that turns these drawers into junk, and you are going to reclaim them for a new and fulfilling purpose. This will allow you to clean out the depths of your home, which will feel like you are cleaning out your deepest, darkest secrets. It is also a wonderful activity for the second day of your challenge because the change is in the deeper parts of your home - somewhere where you won't see it immediately, but you will know it is there. Think of it as a chance of physically rewiring the subconscious of your home.

To do this activity, take everything out of your drawers and completely clean them out. Before you do anything else, decide what new purpose these drawers will serve. Then, you can begin sorting through everything. Eliminate anything that is not useful or does not bring you joy. Then, anything that fits the specific purpose of the drawer can be neatly replaced back inside. If you wish to enhance the organization process, you can include drawer inserts. However, there is no need for these if you do not desire them. Only purchase them if they will genuinely make you feel happier and keep your belongings more organized.

Once you are done going through everything, eliminate anything that you no longer need or want. Typically, junk drawers are filled with smaller treasures that have little to no value or purpose. Unless you have something valuable that is worth selling, simply throw the rest in the trash. In most instances, there is nothing worth donating in these drawers. It is all simply garbage that we are too attached to throw out.

Once you have finished emptying your junk drawers and repurposing them, you are done with day two. Feel free to write about the experience and how it made you feel. Remember, everything you write d can help you process emotions greater than simply thinking them. You will also give yourself something to refer back to, should the transition become emotionally difficult at any point in the future.

Day 3

Today you are going to go a little deeper into your experience. You are going to trash everything that you no longer need. Any items that are broken beyond repair, or that have been sitting around collecting dust while you hope to make use of them in the future should be trashed today. Too often we carry around items from place to place because we fear that without them we will not have access to the benefit that they once offered. Do not allow this fear to keep you from trashing items that no longer belong in your home, or any home.

As you are doing this, take your time. Go into each room, and only trash what you can immediately recognize as trash. Look at your belongings with unbiased eyes and genuinely ask yourself what needs to be eliminated. There is no need to leaf through the depths at this point, as you will go deeper in the coming days. Right now, you simply want to remove the trash from the surface of your home: all of the areas that you can see when you initially walk into the room.

Eliminating the trash first makes everything easier. The process of getting rid of things that you have been holding on to out of fear, guilt, or other unhappy emotions can be extremely liberating. Often, when we are too guilty to get rid of something, we also feel unwanted feelings any time we look at it. For example, perhaps you purchased an accessory for your living room and then later decided you no longer wanted it, or it broke, and you told yourself you would fix it. You might keep it around or store it in your closet because you feel guilty that you invested your money in it. Money is a resemblance of time, so what you feel guilty about is that you invested a significant amount of your time into acquiring that object and then it broke or became useless to you. Now, you don't want to throw it away because you fear that it will resemble lost time, and that makes you feel sad or perhaps angry. Instead, you keep it. Every time you look at it now you will feel guilt, anger, sadness, and perhaps many more unwanted or negative emotions. When this happens, you have now invested time into making money to acquire an object that you don't want, and then you invest time into feeling bad over not wanting it anymore. Some people invest days, weeks, months, and even years feeling this type of guilt over a variety of their belongings. By throwing these items away and being done with them once and for all, you liberate yourself from those negative emotions.

Remember, you don't have to comb through the depths of every room and throw everything away. At least, not yet. In the coming days, you will experience several opportunities to throw stuff away that you no longer want or need. Before you're done day three, remember that you are still supposed to be putting one item into your donation box. Then, if you desire to, you can write about your experience and what you felt when you were eliminating these unwanted and unneeded items from your home and your life.

Day 4

Almost everyone has a guest room, or something similar, where they begin storing items that they aren't using. These items are often things that we never use but don't want to eliminate either. They may hold memories from your past or hopes you had for your future. You may have used an item once or twice and then placed it in the guest room, truly believing that you would use it again at some point but you never did. It is the time that you eliminate these items from your guest room or storage room, and let them go from your life.

This is something that you will want to take a few hours on, to give yourself enough time to tackle the entire task truly. Make sure that you do it all in one day, and that you don't leave any of it for later. Often when we are organizing, we promise ourselves that we will do more later and then we simply shut the door and "forget" to finish our project. You do not want to do that with this room. This room is one of the most toxic rooms in our homes if we are not careful, and you must be sure to complete it all in one day. You might want to take breaks throughout the process, but don't quit until the entire project has been completed.

To complete this task, start in one corner of the room. There is no need to try and do it all in one go. You can take your time and focus on one thing at a time. Start with one box, then another. Work your way around the room slowly. Have designated areas for garbage, donation items, items you want to sell, and items you want to keep. Once everything has been gone through, you can organize the items you want to keep back into respective storage spaces. The rest should be dealt with that day. Throw your unwanted items away, put the donation bin in the car so you can take them to the donation drop off, and post any items you want to sell. Give yourself a timeline for items that you are selling: if they do not sell in seven days, they get put in the donation bin where you are still accumulating your one item per day for the remainder of this challenge.

Once you have completely cleaned out your guest room, take some time to freshen it up. Vacuum, turn out the bed, open the blinds, and wash the windows. Give the room a little life to bring it back from the consumerism tomb that it previously became. When you are done, go ahead and do your daily journaling so you can write about how it felt to work through these items and face the reality of who you were, who you are, and who you genuinely want to become.

Day 5

We often carry things around in our dressers that we no longer want or need. Today, you are going to donate some items that you no longer need to a charity or organization who can then give them to those in need. This task should be fairly simple. Head into your wardrobe with a plastic shopping bag and walk out with the bag full of items you no longer want or need. Let those who need the items have them, and you can find joy in knowing that your wardrobe is now much lighter and easier to manage without as many clothes in it.

Eliminating things that you no longer wear can feel great. It helps you identify who you are, and who you aren't. When we hold onto clothes that we no longer fit into or that we simply don't wear, we become honest with ourselves about who we are. Often, the root cause for us holding on to these items is that they represent who we think we are or who we want to be, and they allow us to secretly wish for who we aren't. This creates a series of negative side effects including several that can be damaging on self-esteem and self-confidence. The best thing to do is to eliminate these items and maintain the clothes you do want and wear on a regular basis.

While you are at it, if you find any clothes that are ripped, excessively worn, or stained, you can throw them away. These items are no longer useful and keeping them around simply to fulfill your physical attachment to your memories is not beneficial to your wellness.

Once you have completely gone through your wardrobe and filled your bag with donation items, put the items in your larger donation bin to be taken to the donation drop off at the end of the challenge. Also, put your daily item in the box. Then, you can do your daily journaling. This will mark the completion of day 5 of your 30-day challenge.

Day 6

Today you are going to focus on loose paper in your home. The primary things you will focus on include: newspapers and magazines, mail, and receipts.

Newspapers and magazines tend to build up in our homes. Often, we don't even read them anymore because we can find all of that information online. It is time for you to take appropriate action with your newspapers and magazines. Today, you are going to recycle everything that you have not read and will not read. Then, you are going to contact all of the places that deliver you newspapers and magazines, and you are going to request to end your subscriptions. Unless, of course, you actually read any of them. If you do find yourself actively reading them as they come in, it makes perfect sense to continue receiving them. Simply vow that once you're done, you will throw the remainders into the recycling so that you do not have them piling up around your home.

Mail seems like such an archaic form of communication these days, yet we still seem to receive so much of it. Today, let's take some time to think about how you handle mail when you get it. Do you throw away the junk mail, or do you let it sit on your counter until it has piled up? Do you shred confidential mail, or do you keep it in a pile and say "I'll do it later"? What are your habits around the mail you receive? Today you are going to go through any piles of mail you have sitting around and deal with them. Unwanted junk mail will be put in the recycling, and unnecessary confidential mail will be shredded. If there is an option, such as with bank statements, you should go online and opt for online communications instead of paper communications. Then, you are going to put in place a new strategy for when you receive mail from this day forward. Whenever you receive junk mail, it should go directly into the recycling. Whenever you receive confidential mail that does not need action, you will shred it immediately and put it in the recycling as well. Anything that is confidential and requires action should be placed in an accessible spot, acted upon as soon as possible, and then shredded and eliminated.

When it comes to receipts, it is important that you stop piling them up around you. If you keep receipts for tax purposes, be sure to have an effective filing system in place and as soon as you come home immediately file your receipts from the day. Any receipts that are not necessary should be immediately discarded. If a cashier asks if you need a receipt and you do not require it for tax purposes, you should request that they simply recycle the receipt for you. This will keep you from having to remember to do it yourself later on.

Paper can overwhelm your home, car, and if you have one, your purse as well. We often accumulate so many pieces of paper that do not have direct importance in our lives and all it creates is a massive amount of clutter. For the paper that is important, we rarely have strictly enforced rules for ourselves for how we will deal with this paper. Today, you are going to change that.

Once you are done dealing with your paper, you can put your one item away in the donation box. Then, you can complete your daily journaling activity. After that, you are completely done for day six of your 30-day minimalist challenge!

Day 7

Earlier this week you donated an entire bag of clothing items. Today, you are going to actually organize your dresser. When you are doing this, you want to make sure that you are making everything accessible in a way that makes it easy to keep your dresser clean. You will also get a second opportunity to get rid of anything you no longer want to keep.

The first step to organizing your dresser is to remove absolutely everything. Then, you want to clean out each drawer. Vacuum the drawer, and make sure there is nothing spilled or hiding in any of the corners. Once each drawer is cleaned out, decide where you want everything to go. Then, fold your items properly and neatly place them back into your dresser. As you are going through, make sure that everything you have is what you actually want. Anything you don't actually want, you should get rid of. This is especially true with underwear and socks. Often we keep underwear and socks that are torn or that we no longer use and end up having more than we need. Now is the time to throw these away.

If you keep clothes in your closet, you should also go ahead and sort through those. Make sure you actually want what you are keeping and that it is all in good condition. When you are done, you can organize everything back into your closet. Color code everything so that it is easy to find what you are looking for at any given time.

When you are done organizing your dresser and clothes in your closet, you are done with day 7 of your challenge, which commences the end of week one. Make sure that you put away your daily donation item, and that you fill out your daily journal entry. Then, celebrate that you have successfully worked through to the end of week one!

Day 8

Wu-Men

There are many surfaces in our homes. For untrained individuals, surfaces are a great place for junk to gather and clutter to collect. Today you are going to start something that you will continue doing for the rest of this challenge. So, you will do it for 22 days. That is, you are going to choose one surface per day and completely clean it off. You are going to remove everything from the surface, only replace necessary items, and organize through the rest of the items to put them where they belong.

You may not have 22 surfaces in your home, but there is a good chance a few will need to be redone. It can take the time to instill this habit in your life and make it easier for you to stick to on a daily basis. The goal is to learn how to put things back in their spot and keep your surfaces clear of anything that does not belong to them. You want to discipline yourself to see that a surface doesn't mean more stuff is being welcomed in your home, but that you are finally allowing for clean space to come in your life.

With each surface, you want to clear it off first completely. Wipe it d and make sure that it is nice and clean. Then, if you are going to place a decoration on it, go ahead. Anything else should be organized and put into its respective spot. If there is anything, you don't want to keep, throw it away or put it in your donation box. Do this over and over with all of the surfaces in your home. Make it a goal that you will leave at least half of the surfaces free of anything, even decorations. Having completely clear surfaces is soothing for the mind and emotions, and you will gain much benefit if you learn to keep your surfaces clear and clean on a regular basis.

Once you are done your daily surface, go ahead and do your daily donation item. Then, you can also do your daily journal entry. After you complete these three tasks, you are done day 8 of your 30-day challenge!

Day 9

Today you are going to focus on organizing your photograph collection. This may not be a major problem for you, but many people have a significant number of printed images that they hoard around their home. Younger generations already have the majority of their photographs on a digital platform only, but older generations will need to work through their photographs and organize them.

If you have printed images, you are going to want to sort through them. Any that you don't want to keep should be shredded, and any that you do want to keep should be scanned and uploaded to your computer, and then the hard copy should be shredded. Make sure that all of the files you have on your computer are stored in various places. You can store them directly on your computer itself, to a cloud storage system, and to a USB drive to make sure that they are all safe. If you have any photographs that you *really* want to keep, you can make a photo album or put them in frames around your house.

If you don't have many printed images, these are likely not a major problem for you. However, you likely have a lot of photographs on your digital storage units. Today you are going to go through all of them and delete ones you don't want to keep. Too often we keep all of the pictures we have taken, whether they are good or not. They take up a lot of room, and they end up filling our online albums with photographs we never look at. Instead, delete everything you don't like and organize the remaining ones into relevant photo albums.

After you are done sorting through your photographs, you can do your daily surface, your daily donation item, and your daily journal entry. Then, you are done for day 9 of your 30-day challenge!

Day 10

BCE. Buddha

Day 10 is going to be an easy one. Today, all you must do is relax. You have done wonderful until now, and you deserve to relax. See, one of the many blessings of being a minimalist is that you have less to worry about in your life. You don't have as much cleaning to do; there is not as much stress in your life because you are not worried about maintaining or caring for as many belongings, and you don't have to work as hard to bring new belongings into your home. Today, you are going to revel in that glory.

Make sure that you spend the day relaxing in your favorite way. If you work today, then spend a significant amount of time after work enjoying peace and quiet. Take time to notice all of the advancements you have made and how far you have come in your minimalist journey in the past 10 days. Breathe deeply, meditate, and enjoy a cup of your favorite drink. You can spend today inside of the house or outside of the house; it's completely up to you. You want to do all of the things that make you feel relaxed. There is no right or wrong way to spend this day, as long as you are entering into a state of total relaxation. Then, and only then, have you successfully completed day 10 of your 30-day challenge.

After this day, you are one-third of the way done your entire challenge.

Even though you are taking a day for relaxation, be sure to carve out time to clear off one surface, donate one item, and complete one journal entry.

You are halfway done!

Congratulations on making it to the halfway point of the journey. Many try and give up long before even getting to this point, so you are to be congratulated on this. You have shown that you are serious about getting better every day. I am also serious about improving my life, and helping others get better along the way. To do this I need your feedback. Click on the link below and take a moment to let me know how this book has helped you. If you feel there is something missing or something you would like to see differently, I would love to know about it. I want to ensure that as you and I improve, this book continues to improve as well. Thank you for taking the time to ensure that we are all getting the most from each other.

Chapter 3: Days 11 to 20

As you enter into the second leg of your 30-day challenge, you are likely feeling many different emotions. Perhaps you realize that this is easier than you thought it would be, or maybe you are finding it is harder than you initially believed it would be. You might feel a mixture of emotions as you enjoy a clutter-free home but come to terms with the practice of eliminating things you no longer need or want. Perhaps there is still some lingering guilt or regret from eliminating items that you no longer needed or wanted but still held great emotional attachment to. Regardless of what you are feeling, if you have made it into the second leg of your challenge, you are doing a wonderful job. You should take some time to appreciate your success and notice how far you have already come. You are doing great.

For this portion of the challenge, we are going to dig a little deeper. You are going to do more cleaning in the deeper parts of your homes, and you are going to accomplish some harder tasks, like getting rid of items you've been holding onto "just in case". This may bring about even more emotions, but rest assured you will have great success in your journey if you continue following each day as it is laid out for you. If you are ready to begin the second leg of your 30-day challenge, then go ahead and start with day 11. And remember, take your time and be gentle with yourself through this process. It is as much about soul-searching and personal development as it is about cleaning up your home so that you have a clutter-free environment to live in.

Day 11

Today is going to be used for two things if you have a family with young children, or one if you don't. If you have a family with young children, today you are going to focus on the toy collection. Regardless of whether you have a family or not, you are also going to focus on your prized collections.

We are going to start by focusing on the toys if this is applicable to you. Go through every storage container that holds toys and organizes everything. Any toys that are broken should be thrown away. Any toys that are no longer played with should be donated. Children often end up with a bounty of toys, many of which they never use. While it is nice to be able to shower your children with gifts and toys that they long for, it also ends up cluttering up the home. As you are cleaning, think about a few activities you can encourage your children to do without toys involved. Perhaps they might go outside and play pretend, or help bake or do household chores instead. There was a time when children didn't have as many toys as modern children do, and in that time they found ways to occupy themselves without having to own the latest and greatest of gadgets and gear. It is beneficial to encourage your children to do this, as it encourages them to have a greater sense of imagination and learn to manage their time properly. It keeps them from having to rely on toys and such to bring joy into their lives and teaches them to create joy in life.

The second task was to go through your collections. Some of these collections you may be keeping simply because you have invested so much time and perhaps even money into them. It is time to really consider how much you like them and if they are worth it for you to keep them around. Of course, if your collection brings you great joy and it is something that you take pride in, it certainly makes sense to keep it. However, if it does not and you simply did it as a pass time and are now no longer as happy with the collection as you once were, it may be time to let it go.

Once you have dealt with toys and collections, you are ready to move into the daily activities that you are maintaining throughout this challenge. Clean off one surface, put one item in the donation box, and do your daily journaling. If you find that your donation box is becoming full, it is important that you take it directly to the donation drop off location. Do not put it in the garage or somewhere else for storage and simply start a new one. We often fail to actually bring them to the drop off due to procrastination, which is exactly what we don't want.

Day 12

You've probably said it before "yeah, I don't really use it anymore, but I want to hold onto it just in case." If someone were to ask you "just in case what?" you might have a generic answer "well, in case I need it of course!" or you might have no answer at all. Regardless of what your answer might be, it likely isn't a good enough reason to keep storing a bunch of items that you are not currently using.

In many cases, when we see these "just in case" items, it brings us guilt. We think of the things that we feel we should be doing, and feel upset with ourselves that we aren't making time for them anymore. Perhaps the items you are holding onto are ones that you once used frequently or ones that you purchased thinking you would use more than you did. The reality is, these simply make you feel bad for being who you are, and that is never beneficial. Instead of feeling bad and guilty, you are going to eliminate these items and open up space in your life for new things that you are attracted to.

See, in life, we have a tendency to change frequently. Often, our hobbies and interests change on a frequent basis as well. As a result, we can end up with many things that we simply didn't use as often as we thought we might or as often as we used to. In the future, a great idea for working together with your hobbies is only to purchase what you absolutely need. Or, you might take a class somewhere local so that you can gain access to the supplies available in the class while also learning about the techniques and skills you need to get good at the hobby. If you find that you are still deeply interested in the hobby after a while, then you can go ahead and purchase anything you feel you need to enjoy your hobby fully at home.

Once you have sorted through your "just in case" items and placed them all in boxes, put them directly in your car and take them to the drop-off center. There is no need to store them anywhere where they will end up being forgotten about and staying a part of your household clutter. You need to get rid of them right away.

Complete your daily activities for the challenge, and then you are done for day 12!

Day 13

Today we are going to focus on some digital organization. Previously, you went through all of your photographs online and sorted through them to discover which you wanted to keep and which you wanted to eliminate. You also went through the process of putting them all into neat folders so that they were organized. Today, you are going to do this with the rest of our online belongings.

Because our online belongings are digitized and don't take up physical space, we often overlook them. We forget that they need to be cleaned and maintained in the same way that our other belongings need to be cared for. Because of this, they can become jumbled and confusing, and we can end up losing things in our online world. This can be just as stressful as losing something in the real world.

Today you are going to go through your email, social media accounts, and offline files to organize them all. You are going to put new systems in place that will help you maintain the organization of these devices, and you are going to strictly enforce new rules that will help you keep everything in this organized fashion in the future.

Start with your email. Go back through all of your e-mails and unsubscribe from all of the emails that you receive from stores. You do not need to receive these emails on a frequent basis; they simply encourage you to feel the need to shop and acquire more belongings that you do not need. You then want to delete all unnecessary emails. With all of the remaining emails, you should sort them into appropriate files where you can easily access them if you ever need them.

Next, go onto your social media accounts. Since our social media accounts often go back extremely far, we don't want to waste any time on posts or pictures. These can remain intact. What you want to focus on are your friend lists. Go through your friend lists and eliminate any friends who you don't actually know, don't talk to, or don't even like. Often we hang on to people on our friend lists because we feel like the overall number reflects how important we are and we attach a great amount of emotional significance to that number and each person on the list, even if we don't actually like them or know them. Today, you are going to eliminate them all and release that emotional burden, freeing yourself up to focus on who actually matters, including yourself.

Finally, you want to organize your offline files. Go through all of the offline files on your computer, make folders for them, and then organize them so that they are easy to find. If there are any that you no longer need, delete them. This frees up space on your computer, and in your mind.

After you are done organizing your online life, go ahead and complete your daily offline tasks. Clear off one surface, put one item in the donation bin, and complete your daily journal entry. Then, you are done for the day.

<u>Day 14</u>

For the last day of week two, we are going to focus on your bedroom. Your bedroom should be your sanctuary. You should feel comfortable, confident, and relaxed any time you are in your bedroom. When you enter this space, you should immediately feel at peace, and like you are in your safe space.

When our bedrooms are cluttered and messy, we carry that as a burden. It increases our stress levels and makes us feel chaotic in our mind. As a result, we often don't sleep soundly, and so we end up suffering physically. Cleaning up your bedroom properly and eliminating clutter from this space can allow you to release all of those tensions and reclaim peace into your life.

To start, look at the obvious. You want to clean off all of the surfaces in the room and sort through everything that you have been storing on them. Then, clear off the floor. Next, clean out all of the drawers. Finally, clean off the bed. If you have a closet, clean this out as well. With each area that you are cleaning, completely remove everything from the space, organize everything, and only replace what absolutely must go back into that space. Everything else should be organized into its new home, donated, or thrown away.

As you are putting your room back together, do it with your comfort and peace in mind. Think about what decorations and accessories will actually enhance the comfort and peace, and let everything else go. Streamline your dressers and nightstands so important things are easily accessible and nothing else can get in the way. Make your bed, but don't replace a ton of pillows or decorations on top of it. These just end up on the floor or shoved aside so that you can access your bed at night. Instead, simply replace what you need and let the rest go.

After you are done reorganizing your room, you can go about your daily tasks of cleaning off one surface, donating one item, and journaling one entry. Then, you are completely done the 14th day of your 30-day challenge. You are also now done your second week of your challenge. You can take this time to celebrate yourself and your accomplishments so far!

Day 15

By now, you have likely found that there are many things in your home that you have considered letting go of but simply aren't able to. You might be realizing how hard it is to let go of the things you love or once loved. Today, we are going to focus on this emotion. We are going to focus on putting a rule in place that will help you work through this emotion in a way that is comfortable and effective.

Today, you are going to learn to sleep on it. Anytime you have something that you aren't sure if you want to keep or let go of, you are going to put it out in the open and then you are going to leave it there until the next day. Sleep on it, think about what you want to do, and then do it. There is no need to get rid of everything in your life. If you are struggling to let it go, sleeping on it will help bring you answers. The next day you will be able to truly decide whether you are struggling because it's difficult to let go of, or if you are struggling because you genuinely don't want to let go of it. Once you have your answer, you can take the appropriate action of either letting go of it, or store it somewhere safe where it can stay organized and remain useful for you.

Remember, the purpose of minimalism isn't to get rid of everything you have and live in barely anything. It is to get rid of the things you no longer need or want and open up space to enjoy the things you do need and want. It allows you freedom from the consumerism life and the opportunity to enjoy yourself beyond your material possessions. It doesn't mean that you can't have material possessions, though. If you love something, but you simply aren't quite sure of whether or not you want to keep it or let go of it, it's time to practice the sleep on it method. You can do this with any and all of the items you have been struggling with until this point in your challenge. You should also do it with any future items that you struggle with.

While you are working on putting this new practice into place, take some time to complete your daily activities. Clean off one surface, put one item in the donation bin, and fill out your daily journal entry.

Day 16

How many items are you keeping because of their sentimental value, and nothing more? Items that a loved one gave you or that once belonged to a loved one, and you hold onto them because of what they resemble you. They might resemble the person themselves, or they might be a symbol of a special time in your life. Old t-shirts, pieces of jewelry, quilts, and more are often kept simply for the sentimental value that they carry.

Sentimental value is a high value, but we often turn it into a higher value than it genuinely needs to be. If you are carrying around sentimental items simply because of their sentimental value and for no other reason, it is the time that you let go of them. If you are not using them and they do not bring you joy daily, or on a regular basis (at least once per week), you should consider letting them go. It is time to clear up space in your life for you to enjoy the things that bring you greater joy than sentimental items.

We often hold onto sentimental items because we feel they are a key to our past. They hold memories or unlock feelings that we worry we may never have again if we don't keep said item around. The reality is, this simply isn't true. You can have any memory or emotion you want without having to have a physical item available to remind you of it. While it can be nice, it can also create clutter.

Having one or two sentimental items is fine, especially if they are ones you use on a regular basis or that bring you joy on a regular basis. But if you are keeping them around simply for what they resemble for you, you need to let them go. If you are really struggling with letting them go, consider taking a picture of them and storing it into a "sentimental items" file on your computer. Then, you can let go of the physical item itself. You will likely feel a great release as you let the past go and open up space in your physical life and in your emotional and psychological life for the future.

Once you are done sorting through and clearing out sentimental items, you can do your daily tasks of cleaning off one surface, donating one item, and journaling your daily entry. Then, you are done for the day.

Day 17

We have been taught that accessories are a major asset to our wardrobe. So much so that we often end up hoarding endless amounts of accessories to accentuate our wardrobe. Massive jewelry collections, hair accessory collections, purse collections, shoe collections and other collections tend to accumulate in our lives as we aspire to be able to create any look we desire at any given moment. In most cases, we don't even wear half of them; we simply have them because we think we may want to use them at some point in the future. It is another classic "just in case" scenario.

Today, you are going to organize your accessory collection. Anything you own that you don't use on a regular basis should be eliminated. You want only to have what you use on a frequent basis left behind. Believe it or not, accessories take up a great amount of space in our homes. We often have so many of them that we end up storing them all over the place in various little boxes and storage contraptions. In many cases, we often even forget what we have, so it never gets used. If you are having this issue, it is time to eliminate them and move on! You need to narrow d your accessory collection to only what you need and nothing more. Let everything else go.

After you are done going through your accessories, you can complete your daily challenge tasks. Then, you are done for the day!

Day 18

Today, you are going to work on a task that might be difficult, but it will also bring great reward. You are going to have an unplugged day. You are going to turn off all of your electronic devices and refrain from using any of them for the rest of the day. TVs, cell phones, radios, computers, tablets and any other electronic devices that you use should all be eliminated for the day. You are going to spend the day doing wholesome real-world activities, free of any electronic distractions.

As a society, we tend to drown ourselves into the world of technology on a daily basis. We are frequently caught up in social media and other online functions as we dissolve hours and hours of time into our electronic devices. While technology is a highly valuable asset in our society, it is also an addictive habit that we must learn to moderate. By taking regular unplugged breaks from the society, we allow ourselves to reset our inner world and have more focus on what is around us. We remind ourselves that there is more to life than the online world, and we are able to reconnect with life itself. It gives us an opportunity to remember what it feels like to live in the now, which can have an incredibly emotional and psychological benefit for our overall wellbeing.

You are encouraged to go a full 24-hours without using any electronic devices today. At the very least, go 12-hours. As you are enjoying your unplugged day, go ahead and complete your three daily tasks so that you accomplish all of your day 18 tasks for the 30-day challenge.

Day 19

The amount of clutter we gather in our kitchens is incredible. We often end up with a number of different gadgets and devices that are used for a variety of different things. Peelers, cork removers, bottle openers, utensils, graters, and several other types of smaller gadgets can build up in our kitchen. We also tend to hoard small appliances that are supposed to make cooking easier. Perhaps you are also hoarding cookbooks, and perhaps even some ingredients that you don't actually use. Today, you are going to sort through them all.

Start with your counters: clear them off and sort through everything you have stored on them. Remember you want to be throwing things away, donating some, and only keeping what you really want and need. Anything you don't use on a regular basis should not be considered a want or need, no matter how handy or useful the device has the potential to be. After you do your counters, go into your drawers. Then, go into your cupboards. Finally, organize the contents of your fridge. You want to completely organize everything in all of these areas so that when you are using your kitchen for cooking, you no longer have to sort through piles and piles of junk. Instead, you can simply find everything you actually need with an easy glance.

Make sure that when you are replacing the contents of your kitchen back into their respective homes that you are being organized about it. Designate a single purpose for each cupboard or shelf and drawer. Then, only return items that actually fulfill those purposeful needs into those areas. You might consider creating "sections" of your kitchen to help you choose a purpose. For example, you might keep serving dishes, cookware and cooking utensils near the stove, dishes and utensils near the sink, and storage devices near the fridge. By creating these different sections within' your kitchen, you make it extremely easy to know where things should be placed. You also make it easy to access what you need from whichever appliance you are working next to.

The final thing you should do in your kitchen is to sweep and mop the floors and clean out your sink. Freshen it up, open the window, and let in some natural lighting. This will help your kitchen feel cleaner and more welcoming. When you are done, complete your daily challenge tasks. Then, you are all done with day 19 of your 30-day challenge!

Day 20

You may not have noticed previously, but you likely store a ton of things on the floor. Look in obvious sight, and look in less obvious sight. You might be surprised to see how many things are being hidden in plain sight. Today, you are going to focus on clearing your floors and cleaning them up properly. Your end goal will be to have floors that can be vacuumed, swept, or mopped effortlessly without having to clean before you do these tasks.

You are going to go through every room in your house to do this. Start in one room, and work your way through the rest. Carry a garbage bag, a donation box, and cleaning supplies from room to room. You want to pull everything off the floor. Throw things away, donate what you no longer need or want, and organize what you want to keep. As you finish in each room, clean the floor completely. You should be able to clean the floor without having to lift, clean, or move anything off the floor. In other words, all of the trash and unwanted items should be gone, and all of the items that are being kept should be properly stored away in their unique homes that aren't on the floor.

When you have completed this task, you may complete your daily challenge tasks. This will mark the end of day 20 and the end of your second leg of the challenge. After this, there are only 10 days left!

Chapter 4: Days 21 to 30

You are officially entering the last leg of the 30-day challenge. Starting today, you will be completing the last 10 days of the challenge, and then you will be done. For the end of your challenge, we are going to be gentle but persistent. You are going to get the rest of your house in order, and you are going to work on your inner world as well. By the end of this leg you should feel refreshed and rejuvenated, and you should be able to look around your house and see peace and comfort, instead of chaos and clutter.

If you have made it this far, you should celebrate yourself. Minimalism is an easy lifestyle, but it isn't always easy to transition into this lifestyle. You want to always congratulate yourself and celebrate your successes as you make any large changes in your lifestyle. After all, if you have made it this far then you are doing a wonderful job. You deserve to feel happy and joyful about your accomplishments and take pride in your success.

Day 21

Today you are primarily going to focus on your daily tasks. You are going to take it easy and focus on your inner world and wellbeing. You are going to breathe, meditate, and take it slow. Remember, this challenge is not intended to be tough or to shock you into a new way of life. You want it to be refreshing, rejuvenating, and effortless. You want to feel good as you complete each task, and feel confident as you embrace your new lifestyle. The easier you are on yourself, the more you will enjoy the transformation, and the more likely the new lifestyle will stick, and you won't end up reverting back to old habits after this challenge is completed.

Take some time today to completely relax. Do whatever make you feel at total peace, and nurture your inner world. You are also going to take some time to look back at your emotions over the challenge so far. Think about times that were difficult, and think about how the end result made you feel. Think about where you have experienced resistance or struggle, and notice what it felt like to work through those emotions. Or, if you are still carrying them, take some time to work through those emotions.

Today is all about taking care of yourself and nurturing your inner space. A major part of minimalism is learning to nurture ourselves and take care of our inner world. It is important that you take the time to embrace this part of the lifestyle change when you are in the process of transforming your life to one of a minimalist. As your physical world declutters and frees itself from emotional burdens and setbacks, it should become easier for your psychological and emotional worlds to do the same.

Take your time, go slowly, and enjoy each part of today. Don't forget to do your daily challenge tasks. In addition, you are going to add a new daily task. You are going to spend at least 20 minutes per day allowing yourself to relax and enjoy the moment completely.

Day 22

The addition of electronics in our world has been a wonderful one, but it has also brought about a great deal of clutter. Think about how many belongings you have that are electronics or that are accessories for your electronics. Remotes, cases, batteries, cords, and more can all become clutter when we aren't actively maintaining them and keeping them organized and properly stored away.

Today, you are going to focus on cleaning up your electronic devices. Any accessories will need to find a proper home, and devices themselves will be stored properly as well. Smaller devices can be stored neatly in drawers, and larger devices should be kept in a tidy and organized space. If you have a TV stand, for example, take some time to organize the stand and make sure that anything on top of it is neat and tidy and is resting where it is supposed to. You also want to take a look at the cords. Do some cord management by tying up loose ends and keeping them streamlined. The more organized your cords are, the neater your electronics will look.

After you are done, complete your four daily tasks: relax for 20 minutes, donate a daily item, clear off a surface, and complete your daily journal entry. Then, you are done for day 22.

Day 23

Today you are going to start a week-long challenge that you will use for the rest of the

30-day challenge. This challenge might be tough, but you can certainly do it. You are not going to spend money for an entire week, outside of necessities like gas and groceries. You will not purchase fast food or eat at restaurants, purchase clothes or other unnecessary items, nor will you spend money on anything else. You are going to refrain from purchasing anything at all this week.

We spend money faster than we make money in this society, and it leads to a negative cycle that can be hard to break. In many cases, we don't even realize how much money we are spending until it is all gone. You are going to start changing this cycle by taking this week off from spending any more money. The amount you will save from not shopping will be incredible.

We often don't realize that we are spending our money. And in some cases, we don't know how much we are spending over time. We buy a shirt here, a pair of pants there, a bag of chips here and drink from our favorite coffee house there. We spend a little bit at a time, and we forget about how much it all amounts to when we are done. It leads to a negative cycle where we are constantly eating through any money we might have. It also leads to using bringing home a significant amount of clutter that we don't actually need. In many cases, the trinkets we are buying and bringing home aren't things we actually wanted. Instead, they are impulse purchases we made that were intended to help us feel better about something in our lives that we may be feeling unhappy about. Stress, anger, sadness, and other emotions can lead us to spend money impulsively. We must learn different coping methods if we are going to save money and refrain from bringing home any extra and unnecessary junk.

So, put your money aside and stop spending starting today. You will keep this up for one week. Don't forget to complete your daily challenge tasks so that you can successfully complete day 23 of your challenge!

Day 24

Today, you are going to be kind to yourself. You are going to spend an entire day without judging yourself or speaking harshly to yourself. You will not engage in any negative self-speak. Instead, you are going to practice working on positive self-talk and start developing a positive relationship with yourself.

With the rise of consumerism has come an even greater rise of self-doubt and self-criticism. We see billboards and major campaigns that show us who we are supposed to be, and when we realize we aren't that person we begin engaging in self-doubt and negative self-talk. We question ourselves and what must be wrong with us, and we fail to be kind to ourselves. It can be extremely damaging on our emotional, psychological and often indirectly on our physical wellbeing. It is important that we learn to love ourselves as we are and be kind to ourselves. When we learn to be this way, we can lead a more peaceful and positive life.

Today, anytime you notice you are harsh or judgmental towards yourself, you are simply going to change your thoughts to "I love, honor, and respect myself." There is no need to punish or criticize yourself for the negative feedback, as this would go against the purpose of today's challenge. Simply be kind and gently direct yourself back on track for your daily tasks.

At some point throughout the day, be sure to complete your four daily challenge tasks. Spend 20 minutes relaxing, clear off a surface, donate one item, and complete your daily journal entry.

__Day 25__

When we no longer have to worry about investing time into acquiring and maintaining our physical possessions, we free up a great amount of time to begin enjoying our lives. Today, you are going to start enjoying that free time. You are going to try something new that you have never done before.

Trying something new can be something small and simple, or it can be something large and extensive. You can do something as simple as trying a new beverage or taking a new class, or you can try something incredible like skydiving or scuba diving. Whatever you choose to do, try and make it something that you've always wanted to try but never felt that you had the time to complete. Or, if you truly don't have the time today to complete that one thing, schedule a time to do it and book all of the necessary appointments you need to complete that task and do something smaller for today.

When we try new things, we open our minds to the world of possibility. We exercise our freedom and our right to be who we want to be, and the outcome can be extremely liberating. It is important that you try new things on a regular basis, as this will allow you to keep yourself from feeling mundane and trapped in a world of routine where days melt into each other and time seems unimportant and irrelevant.

After you are doing trying something new, do your daily challenge tasks. Then, you are all done for day 25 of your 30-day challenge!

Day 26

Today you are going to do another task that has nothing to do with material belongings. You are going to spend an entire day without complaining. For one 24-hour period, you are not going to complain about anything at all. You won't complain about time, traffic, inconveniences, people, or anything else that you might feel compelled to complain about. You will simply appreciate life whenever and wherever you can, and stay quiet and calm in moments where you feel stressed, and like you want to complain about something.

When we complain out loud, we reinforce the negative thoughts we have in our heads. It can create a terrible downward spiral of frequent negative thoughts that arrive in similar situations, and before we know it, we are trapped in negative habits that can hold us back and keep us from experiencing true joy in life. When we learn to refrain from outwardly experiencing these negative thoughts and emotions, we learn to deal with them inwardly in a more positive method as well. The outcome can be liberation from negative thoughts and lasting negative emotions. We learn to embrace life, go with the flow, and accept that not everything will happen in the most convenient manner possible. It is one of the greatest lessons you can teach yourself.

In addition to not complaining about 24-hours, you should complete your daily challenge tasks. Spend 20 minutes relaxing, clear off one surface, donate one item, and write your daily journal entry.

Day 27

Many people hoard books, which can turn into us having massive collections of titles that we have read but will likely never look at again. Books are valuable, and the knowledge they offer us is unparalleled. However, they also take up a lot of space and can become overwhelming and difficult to store over time. Today, you are going to focus on narrowing d your book collection.

There are several ways to improve your book collection, but first, you are going to start with what you have on hand. Start by going through every book you have and putting the ones you will never read again into a donate bin. Even if you loved the book, donate it. There is no benefit in storing it if you will never read it again. Donate the books immediately after you are done taking them off the shelf. Then, organize what you have left.

To refrain from building up another massive book collection, try one or both of these methods: purchase digital books, or borrow from the library. Digital books are a wonderful opportunity to own titles without having them take up space in your physical world. You can purchase any title you want and have it kept in an online library where you can simply read at your will. You can read it on any digital device you have that allows you to download the appropriate reading application to read your titles. Borrowing books from a library is another great option. Some people still prefer to read a physical book, which is fine. However, purchasing books simply to have the ability to read them physically is quite redundant, especially if you will never read the book again. Instead, borrow from the library.

Once you are done organizing your book collection, you can then complete your daily challenge tasks. Then, you are done for the day!

Day 28

Today, you are going to sort through your toiletries and eliminate unnecessary belongings. You might be surprised to realize how much you have hoarded in your bathroom, as we tend to keep all sorts of different toiletries on hand. Hair products, bath products, skin products, makeup, medicines, and other toiletries tend to build up in our bathrooms. If we aren't careful, our drawers and cupboards can begin to overflow, and we will no longer have space for all of our belongings.

Start by emptying everything out of your shower, cupboards, drawers, medicine cabinet and counters and putting them into a bin.

Then, clean everything d thoroughly. Make sure any spills, grime, or build up is eliminated before you start putting your bathroom back together. Next, have a garbage bag handy. Go through every single item in the bin. Anything that you do not use or want should be thrown away. Anything that you are keeping should be stored in its respective home for you to easily access when you need it. If you find you have too many belongings or it still doesn't look organized when you are done, consider getting drawer organizers and caddies for the cupboards to help you keep everything organized and in its designated place.

When you are done, complete your daily challenge tasks.

Day 29

Today, you are going to clean out your wallet and, if you have one, your purse. We often store many things in our wallets and purses that we don't need to carry around with us. The primary culprit is unneeded cards. Club cards, points cards, and even hotel keys or gift cards can take up a massive amount of space in our wallets. In purses, all sorts of things can pile up. It is time to sort through these and organize them completely.

Take the time to go through all of your cards and everything else inside of your wallet and purse and organize it properly. Throw things away, put items where they belong, and take inventory of what you have. If you have unused gift cards or store credit cards, take this as an opportunity to use them or sell them. There is no need to carry these around if you are never going to actually use them.

Once you are done, complete your daily challenge tasks. Write in your journal, take 20 minutes to relax, clear off one surface, and donate one item.

Day 30

For the final day of your challenge, you are going to clean out your car. Our cars tend to become a mobile storage facility that carries everything that we forget to bring inside or throw away. It is time to get a proper system in place so that you can have your car be clean and organized for when you are inside of it.

Start by taking a garbage bag and a bin into your car. Throw every piece of trash away, and throw everything else into the bin. When you are done, vacuum out your car and wash off your floor mats. Replace your scented air fresheners and anything else in your car that helps keep it feeling and smelling clean. If you have kids in the car or tend to carry a lot around for business, consider investing in over-the-seat organizers or bins for your trunk that will help keep everything organized properly. Then, replace anything that needs to be in your car back into its appropriate home. Everything else should be brought inside and organized into its respective spot within your house.

You should clean out your car on a regular basis to prevent it from piling up with junk and garbage that you do not need to be carrying around with you each day.

When you are done, complete your daily tasks of cleaning off one surface, relaxing for 20 minutes, donating one item, and doing your daily journal entry. Since it is the last day of your challenge, you should also go ahead and bring your donation bin to the donation drop off center.

CPSIA information can be obtained
at www.ICGtesting.com
Printed in the USA
LVHW021916110222
710851LV00008B/138/J